Party like a Billionaire:

How to Live LARGE on (Next to) Nothing

By Travis Rabenberg

Dedication

First, I would like to thank Jesus Christ for helping me though this entire adventure. Secondly, I would like to dedicate this book to all of the people all over the world who helped me along this trip, most of all Mom and Dad. Whether you just let this kid from Michigan ride along with you from point A to point B, or if you where kind enough to open your house up to me, thank you all no matter how small the gesture was. I really do appreciate it.

Table of Contents

Chapter 1:
How to Party Like a Billionaire

There is a hidden world only a select few know about. A series of adult playgrounds, billionaire retreats, and grown up wonderlands that few will ever visit, let alone afford. A world of private handshakes and whispered promises and knowing winks and heads nodding in approval, but only if you "belong."

The Cannes Film Festival in France.
The F1 Races in Monaco.
Dubai desert classic in Dubai.
The Moto GP in Germany.
Grammy's in the good old US of A.
The Royal Ascot in London.
The Sydney Hobart Regatta in Australia.
The Boat show in Miami FL.
Partying in Ibiza.

Maybe you've heard of some of these far-off events or exotic places. Maybe you've seen pictures in travel magazines or watched these locations in a movie, wondering what it would feel like to walk the same crystal beaches or eat at the same five-star restaurants as your favorite stars. Maybe a few are even on your "bucket list" of things to do before you die.

I've been to most of these places, and I can tell you, they're everything you've heard about and more. They're sexier, more exotic, more exciting and even more elusive than you could ever imagine, but I'm here to tell you there is always a back door, always a friend of a friend, a wink or a nudge, a password, code or port of entry into these exclusive hot spots… *if* you know what they are.

Look at me: I'm no millionaire, but I've been hopping around the globe, hitching rides on super yachts, swabbing decks, pecking out freelance travel articles for in-flight magazines and, by hook or by crook, I've gone to some of the most amazing places, met some of the most fascinating people, and experienced truly life-changing events… all on a pauper's budget.

And now I'm here to tell you how to do it, as well:

The Modern Nomad

Are you a modern nomad? Is the thought of a mortgage, a garden, and a white picket fence enough to make you hyperventilate? Does checking your Facebook timeline and seeing nothing but baby pictures and wedding photos make you physically ill?

Do you yearn for adventure, the open sea, snow-capped mountains, or the hottest beaches… with the hottest people… the world have to offer? Is a backpack, a passport, and a laptop your idea of your life's possessions? While other kids were collecting baseball cards, were you collecting *National Geographic* or watching the Travel Channel?

If so, this is the book for you!

My name is Travis Rabenberg and I am what's known as a modern nomad. In other words, I basically travel for a living.

From England to Nepal, Sydney to Singapore, from Monaco to Marseilles, Morocco to Munich and nearly everywhere in between, I've traveled the globe, and I'm only twenty-six years old. My business card reads, "World Traveler, Author, and Entrepreneur." Literally, and in that order.

I'm no billionaire, or even millionaire, or even hundred thousandaire, but I am hardworking, industrious, ambitious, opportunistic, and a bit of a smooth talker. I love people, places, and things and that's helped me talk to everyone from salty dogs on freighter crews to supermodels in Monaco to billionaires in Barcelona.

But it wasn't always like this.

Once upon a time, I was a struggling university student, majoring in Engineering. Like pretty much everyone else I knew, I got a job right out of school. It was an engineering job, last man on, and when they started laying people off a few months later, you guessed it: I was first off the lot.

Before getting laid off, I'd put money down on a new car. When I went to pick it up, the owner told me, "Sorry, Travis, I've already sold your car. But... here's your money back."

It turned out to be a blessing from God. That returned down payment became the seed money for the dream trip around the world I'd been longing to take for as long as I could remember. With that money in hand, and some more I got from selling off a few motorcycles, hitting up some friends and, of course, my parents, I bought a ticket around the world and started my epic adventure.

From that moment forward, my life was filled with magical moments and monumental surprises. I'd been racing motorcycles for years, so it was no wonder that everywhere I landed, as soon as I could, I got my hands on a bike and toured the local scenery. Little did I know this would prove to be one way to pay for my trip.

That's because during my travels, a number of motorcycle magazines started to read my blog and publish my stories. Not only did these publications start to notice me, but so did a few companies such as BMW, GoPro, and Pirelli, who were kind enough to sponsor my trip.

While traveling, I started to do some day work on super yachts—boats worth thirty million dollars or more—and once I started to meet people there, I was invited to a few parties. At these get-togethers, the boat owners all seemed very interested in this young man traveling around the world alone on this epic adventure and wanted to hear more.

I was more than happy to tell them, and that's where I learned that billionaires are just like us: a good story will always be welcome in any company and, if you have one to tell, the world is your oyster.

The Benefits of a Life Lived Differently

Why should you ditch everything, like I did, and head out for the open seas, regardless of your bank account? Believe it or not, there are many benefits of a life lived differently.

If you are living outside the box, trying new things, going new places, and meeting new people, then you need to know there are benefits and challenges that the normal person will never get to see.

Look at it this way: there is a ladder that most people work their whole life to climb, one step at a time. Well, what if I told you there was a way to get to the top of the ladder and just hang out with those people who have already climbed it?

Why would that help? Well, if you are with the smartest and wealthiest people in the world, having drinks and enjoying an event and making a real and lasting connection, trust me, you are much more likely to be brought to mind if there was, let's say, a position opening in their company.

Or even if you're just listening to their experiences, it can help you in your own life. Talking to smart, bright, funny, accomplished, creative, and talented people not only inspired me to think differently about the world and how it's run, but how I operate in my own world. Heck, those bright, wealthy, creative people inspired me to write this book.

And that's where you come in:

A Survival Guide for the Modern Nomad

If you're like me, if you've had wanderlust since you looked out the window in your eighth grade geography class and thought, "I could go there," then this is the book for you.

If your first step every morning is to turn on the Travel Channel while drinking your coffee and reading the travel section in your morning paper, then you're in for a treat. And, if you desperately wish they'd bring back Robin Leech and "Lifestyles of the Rich and Famous" and have it run twenty-four/seven/three hundred and sixty-five days a year, then you're definitely in the right place.

Here you'll find what I'm calling "A Survival Guide for the Modern Nomad."It's your ticket to living large – on next to nothing. On the following pages you'll discover:

- *How to Travel the World for Free… or Get Paid Doing It*
- *Where to Find the Ultra-Wealthy*
- *How to Hang Out with Billionaires, Movie Stars, Athletes & Supermodels*
- *How to Get into VIP Parties*
- *How to Hobnob with the Rich & Famous*
- *And So. Much. More!!!*

So, are you ready? Are you up for the adventure of a lifetime? Are you a modern nomad? Do you have what it takes to live large… on next to nothing?

Captain Adventure Number 1:
Formula 1 for Free in Monaco

Going to Monaco can be a bit pricy, but if you know where to look, it can be quite reasonable. Formula 1 race weekend can be even more expensive with tickets ranging from $150- $4,500, not to mention the cost of foods and snacks; food vendors are charging 3,80 € for a small sandwich.

There is still hope for those backpackers who are just passing through Monaco. If you'd like to find a cheap meal, you should head to the local supermarket located near the finish line. There, you can get bottled water for 0,46 € and a foot long sub for 4,70 €.

A great view point for the race is located on the south side of the track along a hill with an amazing view of the action. From this location you can see the ocean, cars, and starting line, as well as the amazing large yachts coming and going from the harbor. There is a large video screen allowing you to follow the action throughout the race course and speakers allow you to hear what the race officials are announcing.

A large number of locals come early to squeeze into a spot on the hill, so set your chairs up early. These cars are VERY noisy, and being in the bottom of a rock valley, the noise may get extremely loud at times, so don't forget to pack your earplugs.

A great way to spend your weekend, if passing through Monaco while the F1 is going on, is sitting in the shade on a nice lawn chair with a bottle of wine watching the race and knowing you are saving money. If the sun gets too hot, you can always take a seven-minute walk east from this location where you'll find some steps.

Head down the old stone steps that have been carved into the mountain and you'll find yourself at a small private pebble beach with some of the clearest water you've ever seen. Swimming out over two hundred meters, you can still see the bottom clearly. Definitely a great way to end a day of racing, watching the sun set on a small hidden beach.

Chapter 2:
Are You Up for the Journey?

You know that part of every flight where the stewardess takes out the safety card and shows you how to put your head between your legs and kiss your butt goodbye in the event of a crash landing? Well, consider me your flight attendant and this is my public service announcement to make sure you're on the right flight.

Seriously, though, while everyone can party like a billionaire, it's not for everybody. Do you know what I mean? Picture this scenario: you're on a yacht, you're all dressed up for the night, and it's an elegant evening, a small party for a few dozen of the best and the brightest from wherever you are.

Maybe you're floating just off the shore from the Cannes Film Festival in Cannes, France. Or maybe you're offshore of an exclusive resort only billionaires and over can afford. Either way, it's an exclusive crowd of the rich, the powerful, the smart, the fabulous, and even the famous.

And there you are, a fish out of water. Or…are you? Can you rub shoulders with the uber-wealthy without sweating through your borrowed tux? Can you talk to a supermodel without flirting, unless they want you to? Can you converse with a superstar about something other than his or her work? (You know, they're on vacation, too.) Can you be spontaneous and witty and savvy and know how to listen and converse about a myriad of topics, and not just make it about YOU?

I've watched SO many good-looking, smart, bright, seemingly astute folks just get star struck and googly-eyed the minute a billionaire or supermodel or starlet or director comes around and then they start babbling and gushing and you can just see it in the person's face that they only want to get away and… guess how quickly that guest is invited back on board?

Never. So you need to make sure you can hang with the billionaires before partying like one, and so that's what this quick, brief chapter is all about:

It's Not All Champagne and Caviar:
Know What You're Getting Into First…

So, this book is all about partying like a billionaire, but let me be the first to tell you it's not all champagne and caviar. I've traveled all over the world for not a lot of dough, and it's required mopping a lot of decks and serving a lot of drinks and kissing a lot of butt.

Don't get me wrong: I wouldn't trade it for the world and I have had experiences that most folks two or three times my age would kill for. But I knew going in that I wasn't a billionaire myself, and that to party like one I was going to have to earn my keep along the way.

So here are some things to think about before deciding to quit your day job, travel around the world, and *Party Like a Billionaire*:

- **Are you rigid?** In other words, do things have to be a certain way, all the time, every day, for you to be happy? If you're crewing on a yacht, for instance, quarters are cramped and you're likely to be bunking with one or more roomies. Can you put on your makeup in a bathroom the size of a broom closet, with three other girls all poking their elbows in your ear? If not, then... you might NOT be a modern nomad.

- **Are you uptight?** Partying like a billionaire means working like a maniac, with all types of different sorts of people, on all types of various day jobs, in all types of diverse scenarios. Some, make that many, of them are rude, crude, and socially unacceptable... which happens to be just the way I like them. But if you're uptight and have a hard time playing well with others, then… you might NOT be a modern nomad.

- **Are you lazy?** I don't mean this as an insult. It's a legitimate question. If you think all it takes to travel around the world on a limited budget is your passport and ATM card, then you may be in for a rude awakening after your first week of champagne and caviar when you find out you're broke and stranded. That's when you'll take any day job, crew any boat, clean any crapper, and do just about anything to keep traveling. I've spent many long, seemingly endless days working for chump change in a polo pony stable or swabbing the deck of some super yacht only to spend that evening partying the night away with supermodels in a Berlin disco or talking politics until the wee hours with a hot shot Hollywood producer. To say it's all worth it would be life's biggest understatement, but I will say this: you can't party all night and work all day if you'd rather be sleeping in 'til noon. And if your idea of traveling is stumbling from the couch to the fridge and back to the couch again, then… you might NOT be a modern nomad.

- **Are you pessimistic?** Finally, ask yourself, is the glass half full or half empty? Because you have to believe this is all possible for any of it to really happen. I mean, you sincerely have to have utter conviction that you are going to travel around the world, meet beautiful and inspiring people in beautiful and inspiring places for ANY of it to happen. And if you don't think you're worth it, or it can't be real, or it takes a billion dollars to *Party Like a Billionaire*, then… you might NOT be a modern nomad.

If you think you're up for the challenge and have the right mentality, let alone personality, read on to discover **The Six Traits of the Modern Nomad**:

The Six Traits of the Modern Nomad

Do the following six traits sound like you? The more qualities you have, the more likely it is you're a modern nomad, i.e. someone who's up for setting off for parts unknown and embracing every challenge, obstacle and opportunity along the way:

1. **Spontaneous:** The very definition of a "nomad" is someone without a home, a wanderer, a free spirit, and a rambler. Being spontaneous is the right attitude to have if you're going to new and uncharted places

because, trust me, you have to be up for anything – and everything.

2. **Fun loving:** You have to have fun, period. Why else would you be doing this? Moreover, you need to *be* fun. People want to be with fun people, that's what all of this is about. Where you're going, who you'll be meeting, why they're there, it's all about fun. If you meet a supermodel on a 226-foot yacht, she doesn't want to talk about her latest *Sports Illustrated* cover shoot or her diet. She wants to sip champagne and put her feet in the Jacuzzi and relax. Same with a big time movie director or a hot shot realtor or finance guy or inventor or software developer. They're there to relax, and if you're not part of helping them do that, then they won't want you around and that'll be the end of your days of partying like a billionaire.

3. **Curious:** Why do you want to travel? Is it just to meet supermodels and hot shot business types? If so, they'll spot that a mile away and avoid you like the plague. Why do I travel? Because I can't wait to see what's over the next horizon. Because I love meeting new people and experiencing new things. Because I love exploring different cultures and learning how people live on the other side of the world. For sunsets and sunrises and everything in between.

4. **Thoughtful:** It might not seem like being thoughtful would be required for parting like a billionaire, but the fact is you can't just be a taker; you have to be a giver, too. I don't mean monetarily, necessarily, but a giver in spirit. When talking to powerful people, they expect a certain level of attention. You can't just bore them with stories about yourself. You have to be up and ready and available and motivated to converse intellectually, listen carefully, and respond thoughtfully. That takes some work, and a giving nature because when it comes to the rich, the famous, the beautiful, the powerful, and the fabulous, a lot of it is about them.

5. **Quick:** I don't know how else to say this, but people who are successful, talented, creative, entrepreneurial, and make a LOT of money are smart. What's more, they're quick – and they don't suffer fools gladly. If you can't keep up, then you'll get left behind… it's just that simple. I'm not the smartest guy in the world, but I'm really curious (see above) about what makes people successful, or interesting, or rich (!!) and that helps me stay on my feet because I'm actively listening to what folks have to say. I also love life and have a big personality, and that helps me talk

to anyone, from any walk of life, from the deck hands to the captains to the passengers to the rich and famous.

6. **People person:** Finally, partying like a billionaire is all about liking, even loving, people. You have to be a people person or what's the point? Traveling is a group effort, particularly if you're trying to do it on the cheap. It means staying in hostels with… guess what… lots of other people, often sharing a room with you. It might mean crewing on a boat in cramped quarters, or hopping on a chartered plane at the last minute with a group of professional golfers, or taking day jobs for little pay and lots of experience with new co-workers every day. And all of this means working with, sleeping with, hanging with… other people. So if you don't like people, I dunno… maybe partying with them shouldn't be on the top of your list.

So if all of the above – or even just a little – sounds like you, read on, because you're in for the adventure of your life!

The Top Five Reasons Why You Should Be a Modern Nomad

Okay, so you're still here. That means you're up for the journey of your life, and I'm glad you stuck around because now you get to hear my five favorite reasons why being a modern nomad is so great:

1. **Think of all the places you'll GO:** First and foremost, being a modern nomad is all about the places you'll go. North, South, East, West and then beyond, that's what I'm in this for. What about you?

2. **Think of the stories you'll tell when you get home:** Throughout this book, you'll read tips, tales, anecdotes, and/or advice from my travels. These are just a few of the stories I've got to tell from my adventures from around the world, and I'm only in my twenties.

3. **Think of who you'll meet while you're away:** Supermodels. Movie stars. Millionaires. Billionaires. Entrepreneurs. Authors. Singers. Stars. Directors. Software designers. Athletes. You never know who you'll meet on a floating yacht, and that's the whole point.

4. **Think about the connections you'll make:**
   Part of the fun of partying like a billionaire is
   rubbing shoulders with creative, smart,
   dynamic folks who can one day help me make
   my own billions. Everyone I meet, in any
   capacity, is another step forward in my career
   as a world traveler, entrepreneur, and author.

5. **Think about the memories you're making:** I
   am extremely grateful for the time I've had to
   travel the world, meet new people, and
   experience new things. I never forget for a
   single moment how lucky I am and, when I'm
   back home and feeling not so lucky, I just sit
   back and close my eyes and think back to a
   sunny day on the French Riviera, a sip of cold
   beer at a tiny cantina in Mexico, the lap of
   waves off the coast of Cannes or the roar of a
   Formula 1 engine and recall the great times
   I've had, the places I've gone, and the people
   I've met. Like the man said, no matter what
   happens, "… you can't take that away from
   me."

So there you have it, my Top Five reasons for
being a modern nomad. If you're up for it, and by
now, you should know whether you are or not, hit the
road, and find out for yourself. Read on and be fully
prepared before you pack your first carry-on bag.

Captain Adventure Number 2:
Renting a Motorbike on the Cheap in Thailand

While on my trip around the world, I decided to go for my own style of jungle trekking while in Thailand, and here are a few tips on how you can take the same trip... on the cheap.

On the island of Ko Pha Ngan, there were a number of off road motorcycles for rent. For a mere twenty dollars a day, you can ride around the island to any of the beautiful waterfalls or beaches. The island has a population of ten thousand people with a number of small towns throughout. If you are looking for an amazing low cost bungalow on the beach and still want some off road adventure then Ko Pha Ngan is just the right place for you.

Enjoy a nice ride in the mountains on a quad or KLX250F. The island has amazing hill climbs with one of five mountains reaching twenty-one hundred feed into the heavens and one of the world's best beaches at its base.

There was a 2009 Kawasaki KLX 250F with a rear tire showing the cords that I wanted to rent. I told the man if he were to get a new tire, I would rent it from him. He said, "Give you thirty minutes, me get tire brand new for you." So I took a short walk to the beach to grab some food then came back to a brand new Dunlop on the bike. I took off out of town with the hope of completing a circuit around the island on what looked like a two track on the map.

After one kilometer and two falls, I had climbed the first extremely washed out hill about fourteen hundred feet high. As I was taking a break, a man walked over, and in a laughing jolly Thai voice, he said, "You professional not many do try this with big bike." After a short talk, he offered me a seat on a chair located just under his house. He informed me that the road I thought I was on was actually a walking trail.

I was disappointed to find out there wasn't an actual trail; therefore, I set off on a clay two-track. While riding around, I decided to check out all the waterfalls that were deep within the mountains. At the base of each mountain, you could overlook and see all the beautiful beaches. It was around twelve o'clock in the afternoon when the temperature reached ninety degrees Fahrenheit which only increased as the day went on. At the end of one of the waterfalls, I spotted a large pool of water that I could go swimming in and cool off.

While swimming, I got to talking to this couple about riding. They had ridden a 1994 YZ200 to this water fall, as well. He said that two years ago he was

*at this island and heard a path had recently opened
up to the Ao Haad Khuat (Bottle beach) which was
only accessible by motorcycle. They invited me to join
them to go check it out and, of course, I accepted
their invitation. We jumped on our bikes and went on
our way, flying over hills, roots, and gullies to get to
the location. Along the ride, there were some water
crossings which did not amount to much.*

    *I even passed a few elephants in the tops of
the mountains who were giving rides to some tourists.
I do have to say, from riding in northern Michigan,
seeing a deer or an occasional moose was not the
same as an elephant. We were keeping a very quick
pace. It was a good feeling to hear a two stroke bike
once again.*

    *When we reached the turn off from the main
paved road; it was a two-track once again. With deep
wash outs on both sides of the trail, there were also
massive ruts running down the face. The mountain we
were on was two hundred and thirty-six meters tall.
The decent was steep and after reaching one point
there was a bunch of mopeds parked. With a sign
reading one hundred baht fine for any moped that
can't make it out. This sign was in Thai but we later
found out that if they had to haul your bike out it cost
one hundred baht ($3).*

    *After a day of riding through the dust and
extreme heat, we were rewarded with the most
amazing beach EVER. This small beach had crystal*

clear water; mountains covered in palm trees that were completely surrounded you. This view was only accessible by bike or boat. There were a couple of resorts located nearby where you could get something to eat.

While we were swimming in this remote area, I thought about my dad and what he always says about when we find an amazing place while riding, "Son, this is why we work." This statement could not be truer. This was the best ending to an amazing day; sitting in the clear water and soaking up the sun.

A thunderstorm blew in through the night causing massive down pours with some minor flooding and erosion on some of the local streets. I was not sure how this would affect my ride back since most of the hills were red clay with crushed coral dirt. I decided to leave at nine o'clock in the morning only to find the roads were not as bad as I had originally thought. I was headed to the North West cost of the island where there was a road sign to a lookout. I took off down a road that quickly became a two-track rather than a single track. It was a long, uphill climb through the jungle on concrete paths no wider than ten inches in a few of the very aggressive uphill sections.

I ran into a couple of places where erosion was a problem. I was really happy I had gotten the new rear tire put on in order to power through the wet rocks all the way to the top. I broke out of the jungle to find a white KLX250F parked next to a small shack. There were three Thai guys and one Austrian guy sitting there smiling.

It started to rain so the guys waved me in to join them in this small shack. It was no more than a few sticks for a floor, about three feet off the ground, and thatch roof. It was a great place to rest after the adventure of getting up the hill. We sat and talked for about two hours waiting for the pouring rain to stop. They informed me that just one hundred meters away was this amazing waterfall that I had to check out.

Shortly after the rain stopped, I headed off to find this water fall. I had two tour guides; a black lab and another dog that showed me the way. It was rather difficult to make it there, but once I did, it was stunning. This amazing water fall with a small pool below was looking out over the jungle to the turquoise waters below. This was by far the most amazing ride I had ever taken in my life. Everywhere I turned there was a picture perfect view to be seen.

On my way back into town, I had a small spill on the ride down the mountain. The left mirror and rear fender got a little scratch, so once I returned I hoped it was not cost me too much. After a small argument with the guy who happened to have the name "Tricky," (should have seen that before), he charged me 6,000 baht which is about two hundred dollars for the fender and mirror. Thankfully, I only rented the bike for twenty dollars a day.

Chapter 3:
How to Travel the World for Free or Get Paid

Here we go!

Now that you've done some soul searching and realized you ARE a modern nomad, it's time to do something about it. Here is where we kick start your adventure with a little – or even a LOT – of "read now, use now" advice you can use NOW to begin planning your own trip around the world.

Don't Let Perceived Obstacles Get in the Way of Your Dream Trip

It often seems like going on an adventure around the world is beyond our means, but trust me… if I can do it, anyone can. Maybe you're afraid you won't be able to speak the languages in all these foreign countries. Or you won't meet anyone nice while on your journey. Or you won't be able to get around easily. And you're probably most afraid you just won't be able to afford it.

I suppose those are all legitimate fears, but in my experience there is a way around, over, under or even straight through each and every one of them. For instance:

- **"What if I can't speak the language?"** These days almost every country caters to tourists, particularly those who speak English. They want your money and in order to get it, they'll gladly speak the language. And, if not, there are SO many translation apps on the market that with your trusty smart phone, you'll be able to speak almost any language in no time. But if you're pressed for time or just want your own personal translator, try this "Travis Tip": Find a local girl between the ages of thirteen and thirty. Typically, they will speak English and probably rather well. Guys will also, but most times guys get lower grades in school and do not practice as often so they are a bit rougher and are also not as friendly to me.

- **"I won't meet any nice people on my journey."** Sure you will. This book is filled with snippets of blog posts I wrote from my journey and every one of them is filled with the great, fun, friendly, awesome, fantastic people I've met.

- **"I won't be able to get around easily."** Sure you will. In fact, the blog post I chose to precede this chapter is all about the twenty dollar motorbike I rented to get around Thailand.
- **"I just can't afford it."** This is probably the biggest reason most folks stay home and never risk taking the trip of their dreams. But not to fret… you're in the right place.

In fact, in this chapter you'll discover a variety of ways you can travel the world for FREE – or even get paid while you work your way around the globe:

Travel on a Yacht (Free)

Most people would PAY to travel on a beautiful yacht, sail the seven seas, and land in exotic ports of call. But did you know that there are actually ways to do all of the above… for FREE?

Here's how: When rich people buy a yacht, they don't have the time, nor are they willing, to just go "pick it up" like the rest of us do when we buy a used car. Instead, they have them delivered to wherever they are, be it their summer home in the Hamptons or their spacious villa in Greece.

That means there are yachts and boats being delivered all the time across the oceans between major ports. And even though they may not need a full staff, someone needs to swab the decks and swish the toilets.

So how do you find such a sweet gig? Well, they don't list those types of jobs on Monster.com, I can tell you that much. But, here's a tip: if you were to, say, hang out in a port and find the local pub where all the crew and captains head to each night, which would be a good place to start. Buy them a drink or two, get to talking, and find out where they're going and if they need any help. You might just find a deep ocean crossing in your future.

You can also act like a private detective on a hot case and go from boat to boat, asking the captain if there is a position available for a deck hand. If you get a little hesitance or the slightest pause, just mention you'd be more than willing do the crossing for free and their response might just surprise you.

I've crossed to several great destinations this way and while you're not getting paid, seriously, you are on a beautiful yacht, crossing huge oceans and landing in great little ports along the way for fuel and other supplies, where adventures are around every turn.

To say nothing of your final destination, which is likely to be a spot you might never get to without working on a luxury yacht. Sure, you will be working the entire time, but you are working for your food and some crews even give you a little spending money when you get there. And most of all, you get invited to the after party for all the yachts once you land. These parties are a great way to meet and greet the rich and famous and make a connection for your next adventure.

Work on a Yacht (Paid)

As you might expect, hitching a ride on a yacht and actually getting paid as part of the crew are two different things. In the first instance, you're offering to swab decks and wash windows and fetch coffee for the captain in exchange for free travel.

But for you to actually get paid on one of these yacht crossings, most of the time you will need experience. Again, sometimes timing – and the willingness to cross for nothing – helps make your case for you. For instance, if you do one ocean crossing for free it makes it much easier for you to get paid on your next crossing.

It's not like a regular job, where it takes years and years to get a paid position. Oftentimes, you can do them back to back on the same trip. So let's say I wanted to start a crossing from California, head to Hawaii and then travel down to Australia. I might cross on a yacht from California to Hawaii for free, then look for a crew that offers a paid delivery from Hawaii to Australia.

But what do I do when I get there? Maybe I find a yacht going from Australia to India and, since

I've crewed twice now, I might be able to get a paid crossing on that trip... and so on and so forth. Fair warning, it might take you two years to circle the globe using this way of travel, but it will not cost you anything to complete this trip.

And just think how glorious those two years might be.

Flights for Free?

Believe it or not, there are even ways to get your flights for free. Freelance writing is a good way to do that. Most airlines have an in flight magazine full of articles from interesting travels – and travelers – from all over the world.

Some airlines will publish your article about your adventure in their in flight magazine in exchange for the cost of your airline ticket. In fact, and this has happened to me, most of the time the price is for one way flight, which works great for your trip around the world.

Working on a Cruise Ship (Paid)

Cruise ships travel to exotic ports all over the world, and offer first-time world travelers a safe way to see the world AND get paid for it! Sure, there's some hard work involved, but some work is harder than others.

For instance, if you can get a job as cruise staff doing things like babysitting kids, doing group or fun activities, hosting parties and the like, you'll be in a much better position to have more free time to travel, enjoy and experience than if you get a job as, say, a waiter or steward.

But even wait staff can be a great place to gain experience, work hard and play hard in some of the world's most beautiful, exotic destinations. Working on a cruise ship also gives you a built-in "crew" to hang, work, play, travel, experience, drink, dine, and dance with.

Entertainment is another way to travel around the world and even make some cash along the way. Cruise ships are always looking for something new and exciting to entertain their increasingly sophisticated guests. If you have a band and you all want to travel, think about jumping on a cruise ship for three months – or longer.

One of the best parts about traveling as cruise staff or an entertainer is that your room and board are covered so your pay is all yours to keep, or spend in those exotic ports of call – or save for your own trip next time!

Freighter Travel (Paid)

If you're looking for another way to travel the world and get paid, you can also hitch a ride on a freighter ship. While not quite as glamorous, or even comfortable, as working on a cruise ship, freighter travel is still paid work that allows you to see the world.

Fair warning: this crew will not be the easiest group of guys you have ever worked with, but like I said, it's a means to an end and still a way to get around the world and still get paid.

What would you be doing on a freighter? Well, since you probably don't have much – or even any – experience, they will most likely have you working in the kitchen preparing food and/or doing laundry and/or cleaning of the ship.

None of these jobs are particularly glamorous, but they are safe and easy and the places these giant freighters take you are well worth the price of admission. Don't get me wrong: you will be working long hours and doing mostly crap details, but remember – you are living, and traveling, for free. Not only that, but you'll be getting paid for your efforts.

Will a Degree Help Me *Party Like a Billionaire*?

Yes, in fact, a degree can help you *Party Like a Billionaire*. (But not for the reasons you think.) Here's why: when relating to the ultra rich, the things that draw you together are more important than the things that draw you apart.

Things like living in cramped dorms and having a roommate who would be out until all hours and then come home and copy your work. Or maybe an epic party you remember with some crazy costumes at a frat party in a snow storm with a cute girl in a mini skirt you happened to be dating at the time.

As trivial as these experiences might sound, they are the things people remember most from four years in college. If you went to school, then you too have had these experiences.

Sure, a degree will help you gain access into a country under a different visa, but it is not always needed. Instead, it is the life lessons we learn that help us to be relatable to the super rich more so than the degree itself.

Captain Adventure Number 3:
Found a New Crew

After weeks of walking the docks here in Palma Mallorca, I finally found a boat. It wasn't easy, but all that hard work finally paid off. Every day I would wake up at seven a.m. and go from boat to boat, which was normally about one hundred a day, asking for a crossing.

I told them I would work for free if they covered my food expense. I was beginning to become desperate. This is day three hundred and sixty-three of my trip around the world. I was given a date that I had to be home for Christmas because, well, my Mom did not want me to miss a second Christmas.

If I did not find a boat in the next three days, I was getting on a flight home. (Mind you, my credit card was maxed out so this would be a "debt flight" from the Bank of Mom.) No one wants to finish a trip around the world landing at home with debt owed to Mom and to my credit card also.

I had been doing some day work on a 1912 classic sailboat where the captain, Julian, was kind enough to allow me to do some work each morning in order to pay for my food. So I had a place to stay and setting out barrowed the dingy to sneak into the repair docks. This was guarded with very large towers and tall gates where they were not allowing any crew in.

Well, if I was going to get on this yacht, I needed to talk to the crew, right? So I took the dinghy around the back to the docks. I met a crew of old Harley riders and after telling them about my trip around the world riding with BMW, they offered me a free crossing.

I was overjoyed! In just twenty-four hours, I would be leaving to cross the Atlantic Ocean on a 68' Swan sailboat. Our captain stands about six feet tall with a big belly and a beard with kinda a jolly smile. He is kinda like a Santa Claus, that is, one who has been at sea for twenty years or more. He was born in America and has an American wife, but has lived in Australia almost his entire life. Before sailing he owned a trucking company with more than fifty road trains running across Australia. A road train is a semi truck with four full sized trailers attached behind.

The crew was composed of one American first mate, who has traveled a number of journeys around the world and become best friends with the captain. Our cook was a Spanish guy in his thirties with poor English, but great expertise as a chef and very nice. The final member of our crew was a fishing boat captain who was also from Spain. I would be sleeping in the forward bunk that was very short, but it worked well for me since I wasn't very tall.

I was overjoyed to finally be heading home. This had been an epic trip around the world and the best way to finish up this trip would definitely be finishing by sail. For the next twenty-one days, I would be on the open ocean catching fish and getting a nice tan, just in time for Christmas.

After this epic crossing all the super yachts finished our trip in Antigua, British Virgin Islands. All the boats were preparing for the big yacht show. There were no big owner's yacht on the island yet when we arrived, but there was one big ass party. All the crews were celebrating their crossing and how lucky we all felt to find a crew.

Most of them were happier about the large check they received for crossing the ocean. This was an epic party filled with stunning-looking people, an amazing island, beautiful yachts, and thanks to Red Bull, the best DJs in the world.

For me, more than anything, it was just an amazing way to finish my epic trip around the world. I thank God for blessing me with this adventure and looking forward to the next.

Chapter 4:
Finding the Ultra-Wealthy

So, now we're really getting to the nitty-gritty of partying like a billionaire: where to find the ultra-wealthy:

Timing Is Everything:
The Best Time(s) to Find a Billionaire

What's interesting about the rich and famous is that they really, really, really like to travel. It makes them hard to follow, but also fairly predictable. They follow the social seasons, and that means there is a pattern to where they go, and when they go.

You see a little of this on the news, like the way some entertainment website will feature a bunch of celebrities like Jennifer Aniston or Beyoncé in Los Cabos, Mexico over the Christmas holidays. Or how you'll see Jay Z and Sarah Jessica Parker sitting next to each other in the front row at Fashion Week in Milan.

So, if you're on the hunt for the rich and famous, and want to plan a trip accordingly, here are some great tips to keep in mind:

- **Know who you want to meet**: If you're looking to meet a certain type of billionaire, or even a specific billionaire, then the more detailed you can be about who you want to meet, the more likely you'll be to meet them. For instance, if you want to meet surf idol, Kelly Slater, get to know the surfing world and where they hold the most contests. Then follow those. If it's Maui one week and Australia the next, now you've got a good idea of where to be, and even when. Same with other professional athletes like Jeff Gordon or Tiger Woods. You get my drift: if you're specific about who you want to meet, or a certain "type" of person you want to meet, you'll get to them sooner by knowing where they go.

- **Know where they go**: So, let's say you just have to meet a supermodel before you die. Well, there are some very definite places supermodels go, such as Fashion Week, South Beach, Milan, etc., throughout the year. Same with movie stars showing up at the Oscars, at Cannes, and Telluride and Sundance. Same with Formula 1 drivers who follow the race circuit, or golfers or surfers or you name it. Maybe you're a software groupie and all the famous gamers, developers, entrepreneurs, geniuses and designers show up at a certain convention in, say, Berlin every year. Now you just need to find out when and… show up.

- **Know when they go**: When is Fashion Week? A quick Google search tells me it's held in New York in February and September each year. A Google alert will tell you exactly when as the next fashion season approaches. You can track any sport, any industry, any celebrity, any genre or niche, just by doing your homework and staying on top of where the rich and famous go, and when.

Again, this is for diehard folks who really want to meet their favorite entrepreneur, genius, billionaire, playboy, supermodel, superstar or straight-up rock star, and aren't afraid to travel to do so. If you're like me, you kind of just follow the wind and meet who you meet, where and when you meet them. I've met some great folks this way, and hope you will, too.

Location, Location, Location:
The Best Place(s) to Find a Billionaire

The problem with the rich and famous is they're rich and famous and... we're not. That means they can pretty much stay anywhere they want, and lots of those places are really, really, REALLY exclusive.

We're talking private islands, yachts as big as apartment complexes, the ultra-exclusive and very elusive private homes of their rich and famous friends, five-star resorts behind very high walls and lots and lots of security.

But... but... they're not in Paris or Milan or Cannes or Maui to stay at home and watch Netflix. Billionaires like to party as much as the rest of us do, and to do that they have to come out sometime. So, how can you find them when they do?

Well, here are a few great places to look:

- **Google it:** You just saw how, in five seconds or less, and on my cell phone no less, I was able to Google "When is Fashion Week" and get an answer, lickety-split. Pretty much anything you want to know, about anybody, anytime, is online.

- **Become a fan:** Okay, so maybe "stalker" might be the right word but, would you have read a bullet point that said "Be a stalker?" If you want to know where the rich and famous go, pick one and then virtually "follow" them around the globe. You can do this by watching for news stories of their travels, following the sport they play, the movies they're making, the deals they're making, such as in the tech or business world, etc. For instance, if you know George Clooney is filming a movie in Germany over the summer, boom, that's a great time to take a trip if you've always wanted to go there.

- **Keep a scrapbook:** The best way to "track" your favorite billionaire is to keep tabs on him and her (see "stalker" bit above). But this takes it to another level when you cut out clippings or, virtually, bookmark stories of where your favorite billionaire is, why and when. You can keep track of, say, Kelly Slater's surfing contests, Jennifer Aniston's vacations or Zuckerburg's employee retreats, track them, cross-reference them on a calendar and, *voila*, next year predict where they'll be, and when. Sure, it sounds a little creepy but… you asked how to meet a billionaire… this is how.

- **Ask around:** In the next section, I'll have some more practical tips for on-the-ground scouting of your next billionaire, which will include how to sniff around the locals to figure out where the "who's who" are hanging out. But a preview to that tip would be to simply ask around. If you're staying at a fancy hotel, for instance, get cozy with the staff and ask if anyone "special" is staying there. You might just be surprised by their answer.

So, again, lots of time and effort but the payoff is meeting a person who could just change your life. That is if they don't have you arrested for stalking when they find your scrapbook. Seriously, though, if *you're* serious about wanting to *Party Like a Billionaire*, you could do worse than to follow some of these tips.

I've Got Friends in Low Places:
Knowing the Locals

One way to get the skinny on which billionaires are in town, who the coolest ones are and where they might be staying is to hit up all the local joints and mingle. Just… mingle.

Don't act desperate, don't be obvious, and don't be a leech. The locals who know where the rich and famous stay typically know because they…

- **Work at the five-star hotel where they are staying;**
- **Are crewing on their mega yacht;**
- **Served them dinner last night in an exclusive restaurant;**
- **Gave them a massage the other day;**
- **Or know someone who does/did…**

They don't want to risk their jobs just because you want to rub shoulders with a famous entrepreneur, thought leader, movie star, athlete or Formula 1 driver.

So you've got to be cool and work at getting this information the same way you have to play it cool around the billionaires themselves. Here are some tips for finding out where the rich and famous are spending their days, and nights, from the locals who would know:

- **Take it slow:** Don't just barge into the local pub, internet café, or bistro and blather on about how you heard so and so was in town and who knows it and what do they know and… just don't be that guy. Or girl. Take it slowly. Go the café, go to the club, go the pub, order a coffee or a drink, sit around, get a little buzz on, smoke a cigarette, hang out for awhile and get a feel for the place. Figure out who's got the biggest mouth, and then make friends.

- **The later, the better:** The best time to get the straightest lowdown on who's who and where's where is to hit the bars, pubs, and clubs later, not earlier. Go when the folks who drive the cars, crew the yachts, wait the tables, and serve the drinks to the rich and famous have had a few cocktails themselves. Then make friends.

- **Spread it around:** Finally, don't be afraid to prime the pump with a few rounds of drinks. Or buy someone a meal, or a few meals, to find out who's in town and where the best places to find them might be. People like people who are fun, and easy, to hang around. And no one minds a free drink now and then.

As you can see, there's a lot of finesse, time and commitment involved in these types of strategies. But, in my experience, they're the most effective – if not the quickest/cheapest – ways of getting the information you want, and being able to trust it.

Thinking On Your Feet:
Why Billionaires Are Just Like You,
Except When They're Not

The one thing that is going to help you *Party Like a Billionaire* is not necessarily thinking like a billionaire because, WTF. More importantly, I think anyway, is thinking on your feet. Billionaires don't like to be bored, they don't like to be interviewed, they don't like to be fawned over and they definitely don't like feeling used.

But… but… this is your big chance to talk to a billionaire. To get some insight you can't get from your favorite barista at the local Starbucks or the dude bagging your groceries at Piggly Wiggly. But you can't just straight up come at billionaires and try to wrestle information out of them. You've got to be smooth.

For instance, let's say you're at an event in Italy. Chances are, there will not be a lot of Americans there. If you meet someone and know you are both Americans, well, that's a small friendship that will occur. You both deal with other countries hating you, you both can't understand the metro (train) system and your phones don't work and neither of you can remember what the country code is for this country.

At the event, you are both absorbing the new accents, trying to understand what they are saying, and both trying to understand where the bathroom is and what on earth did we just order? This is a time when you can catch them off guard and where you can grab their attention. Ask a question you have wanted to ask a very wealthy person that makes them think.

I like to ask something like, "If you could see yourself at [state your age] what would you say to do or not to do?"Most of the time they will respond with something like "enjoy the little things," or "do what you love." But once in a while one will step back and look at you and think and respond with something profound. That is information you can take to the bank. Jot it down send a text to yourself and remember it.

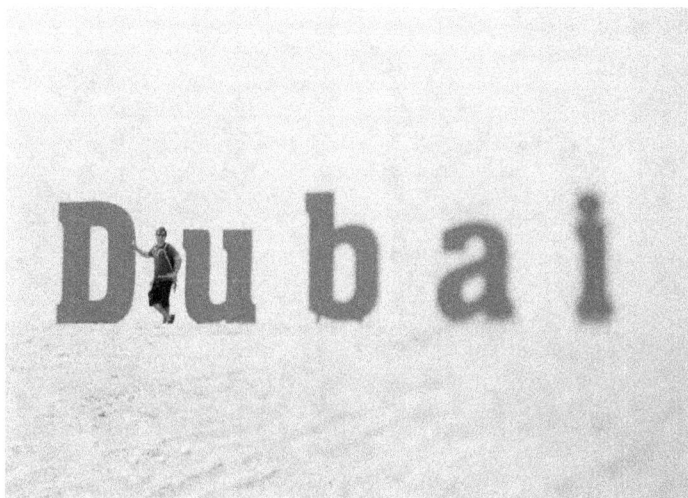

Before skydiving over Dubai Photo by: F.Heden

I took Ruben Faria's factory KTM for a ride in deserts
of Dubai Photo by: Bob Mc Caffrey.

(Top left) Ski Dubia with Matt.
(Top Right) Prince Hamdan bin Mohammed Al
Moktoum crown prince of Dubai.
(Bottom) Skydive Dubia Photo via Skydivedubai

(Top) Marc Comma and Ruben Faria world rally champion's photo by Bob Mc Caffrey. (Bottom left) FX1 Challenge I was driving. (Bottom right) KTM 990 I tested for motorcycle magazine photo by Tonya Colson.

(Top) Camel rides in Dubai (Bottom left) Predjama castle located in a cave in Slovenia. (Bottom right) Hike to base camp of Mt. Everest 17,589 ft Nepal.

(Top left) In Austria meet Playboy Playmate Juliane Raschke. (Top right) At X fighters in Poland with Dany Torres. (Bottom left) In Palma Marrico aboard a 1912 classic sailor. (Bottom right) With super model Natalia Kapchuk at Cannes Film Festival in France.

(Top) Free Hugs event in London giving hugs to make people happy.

(Middle): Having a laugh with Pro SBK superbike racer Troy Courser.

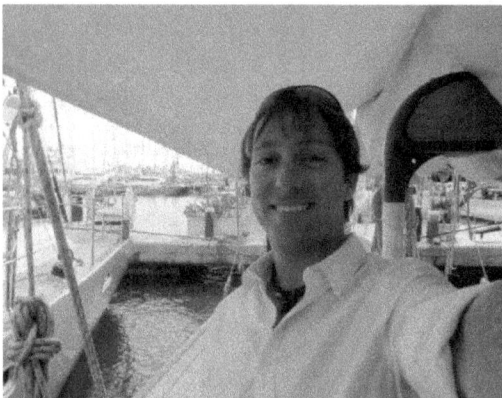

(Bottom): Just a good morning living on a 1912 classic sailboat in Palma Mallorca.

(Top) Poland near the Baltic Sea photo by: Ga Gatek.
(Bottom left) Stunt show in Poland photo by:
Magdalena Krasicka.
(Bottom right) Bangkok Thailand.

(Top) Arriving in Phi Phi island Thailand.
(Bottom left) Rock climbing in Railay beach Thailand
(Bottom right) Always fun to make new friends
everywhere you travel.

(Top) Monaco during the Formula 1 our yacht.
(Bottom) Friends I went to the yacht parties with.

(Top) Photo shoot for BMW and Born 2 be awesome clothing in Poland Photo by: Ga Gatek.

(Middle) Roof top lunch at Marina Bay Sands hotel in Singapore.

(Bottom) TV interview's while in Germany for Cable One and LifeStylerTV.

(Top) Checking the sun set while on the beaches of Portugal.

(Middle) Leaning tower of Pisa while in Italy.

(Bottom) In Vienna checking out the cannels before my next event.

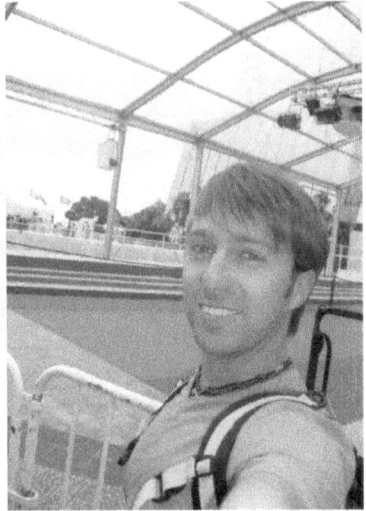

(Top left)Won 4-star getaway to Slovenia in San Marino. (Top Right) Red carpet event at Cannes Film Festival. (Bottom) Riding at Lake Bled Slovenia.

(Top left) Meet Taddy Blazusiak in Poland.
(Bottom left) Fruit markets in Spain.
(Bottom right) Paragliding in northern England.

(Top left) Caught a barracuda while sailing across the Atlantic Ocean. (Top right/Bottom) 21 days crossing.

Captain Adventure Number 4:
Partying Too Hard in Dubai

I went to a party in Dubai with my friend, Matt, who was the owner of a large web page on par with Craigslist. We went to a party with a few girls I meet on the beach that morning. (In Dubai you must have girls with you to enter the bar.)

We started to dance with David Guettaas the DJ. I know, how epic right? Well, little did we know, but my friend Matt came over and handed us wrist bands. We walked up to the VIP elevator with two VERY large guards standing there and headed to the roof top party.

One thing you should know about a party in Dubai is that typically there are not a lot of girls. Instead, they're mostly very rich guys who can't dance or hold their liquor. (In other words, there's very little competition guys.) Once we got to the roof party, the bar was nothing but AMAZING LOOKING GIRLS! I thought this is the best bar EVER! So I started talking to the girls, hitting on them, you know how it goes.

Little did I know that this high class bar not only has bottle service, but all the girls there are, uhhm, how should I put this: part of a service, if you know what I mean?!?

Fortunately, the "regular" girls we were with took me by the hand and led me away from the bar. One of them explained that even though the girls are in Prada or Gucci, they are still a service. I was shocked as I never expected for them to be.

So Matt and my friends all started to dance. Soon after, two drop-dead gorgeous girls started to dance with me and the girls. I loved this: Matt and I and about eight hot girls. On a rooftop party in Dubai on the palm (man made island), sure beats the snow in Michigan.

Shortly after, a tall, older Russian guy came over and grabbed both girls by the arm and took them back to their table. Then he slipped the bouncer a hundred euros to kick me out. I was carried out to the main floor and tossed out of the elevator.

A little while later, I somehow made it back to the roof party and I noticed the girls sitting there were still watching me and my friends, so I motioned for them to come over and dance. So they did so. This made the Russian VERY upset. He came over and told me to leave his girls alone, that he had paid $1,600 to have each of them sit at his table. My response was, "It's not MY fault you're ugly." Note: When dealing with rich Russians, don't call them names. Most of all, don't do it if you are a foot shorter than him and *one hundred pounds lighter (even if you are better looking than him).*

One thing you need to know about the mega rich: to fight someone is too much work for them. Only the poor will dirty their own hands and risk injury or potential jail time for assault. It is much easier to just walk past their drink and drop a pill in it... which is what apparently happened to me.

Either way, I woke up in the back of the nicest Porsche Cayenne twin turbo I have even been in. My head was in the lap of a red dressed blonde Russian prostitute. I looked out the window and there was nothing but sand in all directions. We were in the middle of the desert and both driver and passenger up front did not speak English and were of Middle Eastern decent. All I could think was, "Okay, great I am going to die, but at least I'm driving there in style."

The driver turned to me and said, "Where are you staying?" At this point, I thought very hard and could not remember. Then he asked, "What is your name?" I had no idea. I could not remember who I was or where I was staying. But then, I looked at the beautiful girl in the back seat and figured I would at least die with someone pretty. Then the driver said, "DON'T TALK TO HER." Oh great, now I'm gonna die alone. Crap. We dropped her off at a hotel or building in the middle of nowhere and then headed back to the city.

When we were alone again, the driver said he had found me passed out in the middle of the road just a few miles outside the hotel where we had partied. He told me he was not going to kill me and to calm down. But if I was to throw up in his car he would kill me. (I know it sounds like a joke now but at the time, this man was very, very serious.) I asked if we could pull over so I could throw up. He said, "Really?" I said, "NOW!"

It was at this point that he locked up the tires and slid across four lanes of traffic. I know the tires were smoking because when I put my head out the door to toss my cookies there was still smoke coming from them. I got back in and the driver took me to McDonald's and bought me some food and orange juice. (Neither stayed down too long.) After a little food, I remembered where I was living and my name.

The driver was very kind and said he moved there from Jordan and had something similar happen to him and he did not want me to get hurt so he picked me up. I was so blessed and silently said a small prayer to God thanking Him for this guardian angel. It was at this point I felt really bad for thinking he was going to kill me earlier. He said if he woke up in the back of the car like I did, he might think the same.

I was dropped off at Matt's house and found out that another of my friends had been spiked at the *same club when the Russian were trying to get to my drink. But he was okay. Apparently, I move around a lot when I am drinking and difficult to chase. I am blessed to have made it though this and not had both drinks, where I might not have lived.*

My advice is when you party, remember that big life gets small. It is very easy for people to disappear, passports to get lost, or drinks to get spiked. Remember: I was in a group of friends, not on my own. So never let your guard down thinking you're safe with all your friends. Have fun, but remember: don't let your guard down.

Chapter 5:

How NOT to Party Like a Billionaire

The above story is not fiction. I repeat: this *really* happened to me, this is my life and a great example of how NOT to party like a billionaire. The fact is, all of this globe-hopping and world traveling and crewing yachts and living it up is all fun and games… until somebody gets hurt. And I would never want you to get hurt.

So before we get all excited about the rich and mega-rich and famous and mega-famous people you're about to meet, I thought I'd spend just a few minutes reminding you **How NOT to Party Like a Billionaire**:

We're Not in Kansas Anymore

That night in Dubai could very easily have been my last. I was young and cocky and free and feeling my oats and said the wrong things to the wrong people at the wrong time. But my worst action was acting like I was back in Michigan when, of course, I was in a foreign country; different place, different game, ***different rules***.

Most of the world travelers I meet are fairly young, because this is the kind of thing you can only really do if you're independently wealthy or young and foolhardy enough to head out for parts unknown with a few bucks in your pocket.

And young people tend to act the same way everywhere: loud and loose and carefree, as if nothing can harm them. And it won't, most of the time. But it can, and it does, and so here are a few tips to make sure it won't happen to you anytime soon:

- **Be aware:** Be aware, mostly of your surroundings. If you're new in town and just bar hopping with some friends, and a place looks dive-y or unsafe, this can be one of the most fun places. Then again, if the crowd looks shady then maybe avoid it and move on. If the vibe feels off or strange, get out and go somewhere else. The best way to avoid trouble is to be aware of it in the first place, which is hard to do if you're partying too hard.

- **Be alert:** If you're on a city street, be alert for things that might seem wrong. Walk in the middle of the street, this makes it harder for someone to reach out from an ally and snatch you. Typically, a thief will not want to walk into the center of the road. Watch for the same group – or a single person – following you for blocks at a time, persistent or unwanted attention, etc. That's why it helps to move in packs; the "bad guys" have a harder time conning groups of people, even a pair of people, than they do when you're alone.

- **Be prepared:** I don't want to sound dire, but always have an exit strategy; any time, every time. Know where you're staying, the hotel name and address, and have a way to get back from wherever you're going for the night. It should be with a group of friends, or at least a friend, but if they ditch you and you're stranded, have the name and number of a taxi service; your friends or boss or the hotel where you're staying can give you these.

- **Be wary:** Sad as it is to say, if something sounds too good to be true, it usually is. If the prettiest woman in a room full of male models, celebrities, and billionaires is hitting on you, well, she may expect… something… at the end of the night. If a table of guys keeps offering you drinks all night, well, they may not be entirely "free," if you know what I mean.

- **Be careful:** Finally, just… be careful. All of the above tips are a variation on that theme, of course, but in case it hasn't sunk in by now… be careful. Trust your gut. If your instincts are telling you to run, or at least leave, or turn around or whatever, follow them. Particularly in a foreign country where you're not familiar with things, sometimes all you have is your gut: so follow it, even if it's not always the "fun" thing to do.

It's not about walking around under a gray cloud, expecting doom and gloom and to be attacked at every moment. But the rest of the world is not like Main Street, USA; it just isn't.

Bad things *do* happen to good people, and especially when good people make bad decisions. So make moral decisions, play it smart, and, above all, play it safe.

How to Lose a Really Good Sponsor in a Really Bad Way

If you take my advice, many of you will likely be traveling around the world, partying like a billionaire on somebody else's dime. Maybe you're…

- **On the payroll of some in-flight magazine or travel website, who's hired you to write a story or profile of an exotic locale;**
- **Crewing for a yacht where you're expected to work regular hours on certain days/nights;**
- **Being sponsored by a surfboard manufacturer or skateboard magazine or dirt bike company because of your sports skills...**
- **Etc.**

Either way, you're basically an employee and your employer will expect you to act like one. And, since you're young or fresh or eager or naïve or it's your first time in a new country or city – or all of the above – you'll forget about the employee part and just pretty much act like an ass. At least, that's what happened to me, with some pretty ugly consequences:

When I was being sponsored by a certain, very popular energy drink, we went out to celebrate my new sponsorship in east Germany. It was just after the MotoGP round in Sachsenring, and I decided to go drinking with British guys who are easily one hundred pounds heavier than me. There we were, doing round after round of Russian vodka shots, and of course it didn't end up well.

Not only did I puke on the owner's car, but at some point I called the PR manager's wife ugly. The next morning, I woke up to find my contract for five thousand pounds (Roughly $10,000 at the time) torn in two and told to get out of the company's hospitality tent.

This was the longest, worst hangover "walk of shame" back to my tent on the outskirts of the track. I had a total of $158 to my name and just ten hours earlier, I had it made, my stress was over, I thought I could relax. Now, I was alone and stranded in a foreign country, wondering how I was going to make it through the rest of the month, let alone get back home…

What I learned from that rather nasty, ugly, and unfortunate experience is that, if you're in a foreign country on someone else's dime, you have to act like an employee, not an ass.

That being said, here are a few tips for keeping things professional when you're partying abroad:

- **Know Who You're With:** Always, always, always party with friends. I mean, it's one thing to hang out in the lobby bar of your hotel if you're just in the mood for a quick nightcap and then it's up to your room, or having a spot of coffee at the café around the corner from your hostel, but if you're heading out for a night on the town, in a new and familiar place, use the "buddy system" and go with someone you know and trust. The hairiest nights of my life have been when I've either gone out alone or been left alone, and the trouble(s) I got into would have, could have, been easily avoided if a buddy had just said, "Travis, take it easy," or "Don't drink that," or "Let's go!"

- **Know Where You're Going:** Always, always, always know where you are before you take that first drink. Have a designated driver, know which way it is back to your hotel or have a ride set up already, like the taxi driver that took you there. Back home, we all know where we're going. But if it's your first night in port, you may forget what the streets look like and how to return to your hotel if your friend gets lucky and leaves you stranded at the bar.

- **Know Why You're There:** Is it a professional thing, like maybe a meeting with the editor of the blog or magazine you're writing for? Or is it just a fun, quick, loose night out after a long night at work? The quickest way to get kicked out of a bar, into a fist fight, or out of a contract (see above) is to mix too much pleasure with the wrong business.

- **Know What Kind of a Night It's Going to Be:** Are you the designated driver (DD)? Or are you at an English pub around the corner from your hotel? Having lived and learned through more than a few scrapes, I never go out anymore without at least a rough plan, or sketch, of what the night might look like. If I'm brand new in a place, don't know my way around yet or am the DD for the group I'm with, I'll take it light; that's my night. If it's a place I've been before, I know the locals – or at least know they're friendly – and where I am and how to get back, I'll cut loose a little more. But you've got to have a plan before your first drink, not after last call.

- **Act Accordingly:** Finally, depending on who you're with, where you're going, why you're there, and what, or how much, you're drinking… act accordingly. If you're with new friends you met on the beach and don't have to act professional, let your hair down. If you're with the CEO of the company that's sponsoring your trip and making all this possible, stick to a "two drink maximum" and take the night light to ensure that you can still

Party Like a Billionaire when the meeting is over.

The fact is, it's not that hard to stay in control if you remember what's at stake. If you're lucky enough to be traveling around the world on somebody else's dime, either writing for a travel magazine or crewing for a yacht or just thanks to a loan from your folks, respect that and act accordingly.

Parting Words About How NOT to Party Like a Billionaire

As you can see, there's nothing in this chapter that says: Don't go out. Don't have fun. Don't make new friends. Don't sightsee. Don't go new places. Don't try new things.

All I'm saying is, DO all those things… but be careful, be aware of your surroundings and, above all, be wary. All things considered, the world is a big, beautiful and, occasionally, dangerous place. But the more care you take to look out for yourself, the less dangerous it becomes – and the more fun you can have.

Captain Adventure Number 5:
Yacht Crashers

Monaco was having the F1 races at the time. I found two good looking girls from my hostel who wanted to go with me to check them out. A third girl from Canada named Stephany also decided to join the group heading to Monaco.

We headed out around seven p.m. and arrived at eight p.m. We walked to the top of the hill and sat on the hand rail and drank our 3,00€ wine overlooking the port, as well as the race track.

This was just an amazing place to sit, where the breeze was blowing fresh sea air in and the mega yachts where moving in getting ready for the parties for that night. After the drinks, we walked down the hill and started to walk through pit lane. There were four or five pit parties going on where we walked into the Lamborghini after party VIP section with the girls. In this section, you still had to buy your drinks, so I could not understand why everyone was so excited to be in the VIP area when there was nothing different besides the red rope.

Here we met two crew members from the yacht Mach 1 who were very intoxicated and getting hit on by two very old ladies. This was just outside the VIP area because inside, there was nothing but yacht crew members and deck hands that had the night off and were living it large (or so they thought).

This party was starting to get boring for Stephany and I, but the other two young American girls who were getting hit on by the crew and having drinks bought for them thought it was great and they wanted to stay. Steph and I had a little buzz on and decided to walk the docks and see what yachts had a party going on. So we went to the largest one and the crew said to head down to *African Cat* where there was a live DJ and loud music.

We walked past very nervous seeing the large bouncers on both the rear and at the end of the ramp of the dock. But, we were young and buzzed and had nothing to lose, so we decided to act the part, walk on and see what would happen.

That is exactly what happened: we walked up, took our shoes off, and walked right on the boat, no questions asked. The bartender came and made our drinks and we had some snacks and sushi. We where there talking to a few people for probably close to a half hour before the bouncer asked me who I knew there. With more confidence than I really felt I said, "The owner of the yacht, go and ask him." (I knew he would never bother the owner of the yacht during his party.)

So as I waited, Steph decided it would be best if we just left. "We have had our fun," she said, and I agreed, so that was exactly what we did. Walking back to the hostel, we thought that the last train was at 12:15 a.m., but when we were a hundred meters from the train it started to move. This was not good since the next train was at 6:15a.m., which proved to be very upsetting for Steph.

I did not know that she was a perfectionist and if one plan was changed it was the end of the world. So after taking an hour of abuse and yelling at how I walked too slowly and walking all over the place a police officer told us there were two more buses heading out and we could get the next one leaving in fifteen minutes. We hoped the bus and forty minutes later we were back at our hostel with an amazing story to tell...

Chapter 6:

Talking the Talk, Walking the Walk –
How to Mingle With the Rich & Famous

So, here's where we get to talk about something I really like to talk about, which is… talking. No, seriously though, a BIG part of partying like a billionaire is, essentially, learning how to talk one. Something I've discovered about the rich, the famous, the bold, the beautiful, and the billionaire is that they all love to talk.

Yes, sure, a lot of them like to talk about themselves, but the most interesting, most fascinating, and most friendly actually DO want to talk to you, about you, about what you know, what you've seen, what your life is like in relation to theirs.

Most of us think if we get the chance to talk to a billionaire, we'll really want to quiz them about:

- **How they became successful**
- **Their daily habits of success**
- **Where they get inspired**
- **Who inspires them**
- **What it's like to meet "so and so"**
- **What Bill Gates is like**

But what I've found is that, while they do enjoy giving advice, they also like to quiz other people. You, me, the deck hands, the bartenders, the waitresses, the baristas, the newspaper vendors… we are the billionaire's shared link back to the common man.

By that I mean, their worlds are so insulated that, when they do get the chance to talk to someone like you or me, a lot of them see it as their opportunity to connect – or re-connect – with the real world, which is something they don't get to do very often.

So it can, and should, be a two-way street, a real opportunity, and a real conversation, that you can both enjoy. But it takes some practice, and that's what this chapter is all about:

The Billionaire Mindset:
Get Used to It

The first way to get ready to talk to a billionaire is recognize that, while they may look human, they are not regular humans. They don't go out and buy a gallon of milk, or sit in the Laundromat in their boxer shorts, or "binge" watch *Breaking Bad* on Netflix like the rest of the world.

They are busy with very demanding schedules and lots of people to see and places to go and things to do, most of them business-related. So while they may look like you and me, and even try to "act" like you and me in a social setting, their lives are very much different from yours and mine.

And that's okay because the things we want and need from them – that exclusivity, that world they live in, the people they know and hang out with, the money they've made – are the reason they want to hear from us what it's like "out there," in the real world.

So be confident when you approach someone, but also be aware that they come from a very different world than your own. Above all, be open and honest. I'm not saying to start right out of the gate being fun and kooky, but once you've been introduced and if you're sharing a quiet, calm, or intimate moment, don't be afraid to be yourself.

After all, that's what makes you so unique in the first place...

The Top Ten Topics ALL Billionaires LOVE to Talk About (Know These!)

Now, there are a few things – well, ten actually – that I have discovered almost ALL billionaires love to talk about. If you know a couple of these, or even one, you'll have a common point of reference. But the more of these areas you're familiar with, and especially comfortable with, the easier it will be to talk to your friendly billionaire:

Sports

No matter how rich you are, you will still like the Chicago Bulls or the Detroit Red Wings just as much as any other fans out there. It doesn't matter if he has box seats for every game or if you are just watching it on TV in your underwear back home, sports are a level playing ground that almost every billionaire loves to talk about. (That is, unless he owns the team.)You can talk about how terrible Game three was or how amazing the playoffs of 2010 where. This is a great area to find the same interests in.

Wisdom

I know this is a strange topic, but I've found that no matter how many times I have met a successful person, they always wish to tell me nuggets of wisdom they have learned along the way. And I am very pleased to hear it whether they say, "Don't fall in love for beauty," or "Always bet on black." This information can be abstract and feel like it has no meaning at the time, but someday you will understand what they said and put it to heart.

One thing I always make sure to ask is: *If you see yourself at (state your age) what advice would you tell your younger self?*

This question will make them sit back and think almost every time. They have to think of what they were doing when they were, let's say, twenty-five. It brings back memories of a car that would not start, or that amazing girl he fell in love with. Sometimes they just respond with something generic like "live life," but every once and a while they give you an insight into their life and that information you can take to the bank.

Models

No matter what, there will always be a model nearby at these parties. Now, either she is married to one of the old timers sitting across the table from you or she is the daughter of one of these guys. But nevertheless, they are always around and these rich guys will always have an opinion about them. The good news is, so will you.

NOTE TO GUYS: Models are great accessories to any party, but they can also be a distraction. Try to remember, you're not here to hook up, you're here to network. I have been invited onto beautiful mega yachts in Monaco during the Formula 1 races just because I had two beautiful girls with me. I did not hit on them, I just asked if they would like to party on a boat.

So they came with and the guys were impressed, but once they started talking, the girls lost their appeal. That is where your personality steps in and boom! You have their attention and opportunity.

Boats

Almost all of the rich people I know either own a boat or go out on their friends' boats. This may be a passion of yours, or you may have to study up on it, but it's probably a good idea to at least get familiar with some basic brands and terminology (port and starboard) just in case.

Always remember they were not always sailing a one hundred-foot boat, but that they started out in a Lido just like you. If you don't sail, you can buy one for a few hundred dollars and learn to sail. They will think back when they first raced them and always have a good story. Just because you don't own a big boat does not mean you both don't share the same passion.

Travel

Billionaires love to talk about their favorite countries. And, if you have traveled a little or a lot, chances are that you have already been there. If it is not a location you have been, you can generally kick off a great discussion by asking them why it is so amazing. What did they like? And can I go there, too? This will grab their attention as they sing praises of their amazing adventures through their favorite little country.

If you HAVE been there, it's important to think back to something small you enjoyed or remember, like a taco stand in Byron Bay, Australia or a Water Bar in Rome. These are places, smells, tastes you remember being at and they, too, will remember that street or location to help have a common interest. When traveling, try to not only explore the tourist locations, but also meet some locals and ask them where a good place to visit on a certain night is.

Books

This may or may not tie into the "wisdom" piece, above, but many billionaires enjoy a good book now and then. They may not have time to read a bunch, but when they do they may enjoy a solid business book, a spiritual guide or sometimes just a flat-out murder mystery or espionage thriller.

Speaking about a book before researching the author can make you look dumb. I once spoke about a book on finance I read and thought it was amazing. They billionaire looked at me and said, "Before that author published his book he was worth ten thousand dollars, not a million." So always have good information before blurting it out (like I did).

Movies

It's crazy, but people everywhere love movies, and you'll never know what kind. Some snooty billionaires will only, and can only, talk about foreign movies, nature documentaries, stuff like that. But I meet folks all the time who can talk about the latest Adam Sandler or "Hangover" movie and quote every line.

Favorite movie? Well, sometimes it's not the latest movie that grabs their attention. Most billionaires are very busy and if a friend is not in the film there is a good chance they will not see it until they are on an airplane crossing the Atlantic and it's onboard. So think back to like *Captain Ron*, a movie out of the 80s or something else you remember. You never know, they just might have liked that movie, too.

Food

People like food. A lot of billionaires are "foodies" simply because they can go anywhere, eat anything and the more exclusive, rich or luxurious it is, the more appealing it can be to them. So if you are a foodie, too, or know of a particularly good dish or restaurant or hidden gem of a café where you're presently located, don't be afraid to share.

Wine

This is a big topic for rich folks. They love, love, LOVE their wine. Wine cellars, wine stewards, vintages, grapes, many of them will own vineyards or collections that cost as much as your parents' house.

Social Media (aka Facebook/Twitter/Instagram, etc.)

No matter what, they will have an option on the topic of social media. And, what's more, this is one topic that you can for sure relate to. One thing everyone hates is how often Facebook is updated and you can't find a thing on it. Or maybe how their new iPhone is no longer working here in France, but in Spain it works just fine.

These are things you and I both struggle with and no matter how rich they are, they will, too. If you hear them complaining about how their messages won't open, offer to help them with their account. A lot of times they will be very happy when you are able to close an app or get Wi-Fi when no one on their staff could. Saying, "I have wanted to close that thing for months. Thanks I have someone I would like you to meet." And there you go, suddenly you're on a level playing field.

So there you have it. No matter what your interests, hobbies or passions, chances are you'll find some intersection with a high-powered billionaire. The key is to kind of let them take the lead, see where the conversation is going and adjust accordingly.

The Rules:
Basic Do's & Don'ts of Partying with Billionaires

Now that you know what you'll be talking to all those billionaires about, let's make sure you get the chance by offering you a complete set of Do's and Don'ts for how to Party Like a Billionaire:

- **Do**: *Be yourself.*
- **Don't**: *Act like an idiot.*

- **Do**: *Show the proper signs of respect and admiration.*
- **Don't**: *Be so star struck you can't form a sentence or, alternately, won't shut up.*

- **Do**: *Have an opinion.*
- **Don't**: *Shove it down people's throats.*

- **Do**: *Know proper table manners.*
- **Don't**: *Draw a ton of attention to them.*

- **Do**: *Have a lot to talk about.*
- **Don't**: *Say it all at once.*

It's not so hard once you get used to it, but there is definitely an aura of power and privilege around billionaires, and sometimes approaching them can be intimidating. Hopefully these simple "Do's" and "Don'ts" will help next time you're in the company of greatness.

You Will Always Have Something in Common With a Billionaire:
You Just Have to Find Out What

The bottom line when talking to anyone, the super rich included, is to simply be yourself. Or, should I say: be your "best" self. In other words, be your smartest, nicest, funniest, kindest, most eloquent, grateful, and empathetic.

The one thing you have going in your favor is that, unlike trying to get in to see a busy billionaire, say, at their corporate office or some trade show in the States is these guys are generally on vacation, or some kind of working vacation, when you're running into them on some party on some yacht.

That may be why the rich lower their guard when outside the USA. They're a little more relaxed, have a little more time, and are a little more open to meeting new friends, particularly after a drink or two.

So before we close out our chapter on talking to billionaires, here are a few final trips for conversing with the rich, the fabulous, the beautiful and the famous:

- **Get an introduction:** The best way to approach a billionaire is through an introduction from someone they already know, a handler, friend or spouse, or even a new friend.

- **First impressions count:** Always try to make a positive, friendly, and humble first impression, regardless of how you're meeting them. Even at a busy party, most billionaires will remember a good first impression. But they'll always remember a bad one more.

- **Don't read from a script:** Be yourself and talk about what comes up naturally, without forcing a script or sounding too rehearsed – even if you are.

- **Know when to walk away:** When you've had a good time chatting to a billionaire, know that their time is valuable and when it's over, it's over.

Chapter 7:
How to Get Into VIP Parties

So, here it is, the moment you've all been waiting for: the definitive, ultimate, hands-on guide for How to Get Into VIP Parties. In this chapter I'll share all my tricks of the trade, everything I've learned on my tours around the world about crashing the hottest, most happening parties on the planet.

Now, for you ladies out there, I'll start out with…

How to get to the VIP parties as a GIRL

Now, when it comes to gaining access to VIP parties, I do believe you ladies have it much easier than the guys have. Still, hot as you may be, there are some specific tips, tricks, strategies, and tactics you'll want to follow to get into that next VIP party.

Luckily, I've laid out a step-by-step strategy, from pre-staging to post-party crashing, for you below:

1. **Less is more:** When it comes to getting dressed, sexy is good, but stay classy. There are tons of sexy girls all around billionaires, but if you can stay classy as well, you'll be a real stand out.

2. **Strength in numbers:** Next, find a group of at least three to four friends to hang out with. (And make sure they follow Step 1 as well.) It will always draw the right kind of attention if there is a group of you.

3. **Two drink maximum.** This small, sexy group of you should have a few drinks to start off the night. But make sure not to get distracted and just stay where you are. Put a "two drink maximum" on your partying. Remember, you mission for the night is the VIP or that mega yacht with the big deck party.

4. **Act the part.** Perception is everything. Trust me, if you are a group of hot, young girls dressed sexy-classy, you will get invites. But you never want to look like that's what you're there doing. Instead, act the part. Walk right past a yacht, acting like you are heading to another party. If there are a people on deck, most of the time someone will say something as you pass.

5. **Keep your options open.** Always remember that the night is young, no matter how late it might be. So agree to come onboard only for a little while and mention in passing that you "still have another party to go to." If you are having a good time and think this is the party where you'll finally make some connections, simply act like you have received a text message, and now you can stay and enjoy this event.

6. **Connections first, Courvoisier second.** Remember that your mission is not to just get smashed on free top-shelf liquor, but it is to make the connections to get an invite to the next bigger event. So be charming, reserved, and draw attention but not too much. You can get smashed anytime, but you can't always sit on a billionaire's yacht with your wits about you while everyone else gets smashed. There's real power in staying sober, alert, and charming when in the company of the rich, powerful, and connected.

7. **Keep your eyes on the prize.** Honestly, from what I have seen firsthand, the hardest part of crashing a VIP party as a girl is not to get distracted by the cute crew members or bartender. Remember, you are there for the big fish.

So there you have it, seven simple tips for getting into VIP parties as a girl. Remember, VIP comes first, party second. If you're there to have a good time, great, but if you've read this far in the book I'm guessing you want more than just a good buzz but great connections; to the next party, your next mentor or even your next opportunity. So if that's the case, keep your wits about you and treat getting into VIP parties like a job, and party later.

Now, for the guys:

How to get to the VIP parties as a GUY

So, I mentioned earlier that guys have it a little bit harder than girls when it comes to getting into a VIP party. And here's what I meant: as a guy, you probably aren't going to be able to just walk right up and be invited to the front of the line or onto the biggest yacht. So as a guy, you just have to think more creatively and have a simple strategy.

The following tips should help:

1. **Go on a scouting mission.** Earlier in the afternoon, take a stroll through the marina. I would walk around looking for a stunning yacht next to a very large yacht. (The reason for this will become clear in Step 3.) If I see someone outside, I stop and talk with them. Normally the owner is an old guy who is there with his buddies having a good time. After some polite conversation, I ask the owner if I were to bring, let's say, six beautiful girls by that night, would he let us party on his boat? What guy would say no to this offer, right?

2. **Find some arm candy.** Next up, find a group of good looking girls. Ask them, "Would you like to party on a super yacht?" Of course they will say "yes." So I tell the girls I will come pick them up later that night and to be sure to look sexy with heels.

3. **Double your fun.** After picking the girls up for the night, our small group goes to the boat and starts chatting it up, having a good time. Now, here is why you always find two awesome boats sitting next to each other: ninety percent of the time, the boat next door sees our fun little group and invites us onto their boat for a party the next night.

4. **Networking refined.** Now, the point of all of this is to make connections, so by moving from one boat to the next, and the next, you're increasing your odds of meeting that one special person who might be able to help you. All of this starts to grow and, eventually, someone knows someone who wants to meet you.

5. **Bonus tip:** This same tactic can work for getting into big clubs also (just make sure your girls don't decide to just ditch you once you get them in).

6. **Bonus Hint:** Remember, you're there to network, not get numbers. It is hard to ignore the models, trust me, I know, but keep your eye on the prize. These old timers get tired of dumb blondes talking and are interested in someone who has a story, has passion, someone on a mission and now is your chance. Capture their attention.

Again, I've been invited to a ton of VIP parties and I'm a guy, so take it from me: it can be done. You just have to get creative and work a little harder than the girls. But then, what's new right?

On the Inside:
How to Act Once You're in the VIP Party

Congrats! You're inside. But your work isn't done yet. This event is more of a mission for you than just a party and another opportunity to drink. If you view it like a job, or even a mission, your results will be much better. Don't get me wrong; this should be fun, but it's also more than that, too.

So take a drink and relax a little, but remember you're working, you're not there to get smashed. With that in mind, here are some simple tips for working the party once you're inside (these all work whether you're a girl or a guy):

- **Take your time and scope out the scene.** Look around and see who is standing alone. Do they look like they might own the yacht? Or maybe a big VIP? Sometimes picking the fakes from the flash is difficult. But normally the older, quiet, confident type tend to be the ones in charge.

- **Make your move.** Walk right up to them, introduce yourself and shake their hand. Make sure to give them one hundred percent eye contact. This is the first stage in making a great impression and you want to do it right.

- **Be confident.** Powerful people are confident, and they are drawn to other confident people. So confidence is a key that will draw their attention. Stand tall and be assured in whatever it is you do or who you are.

- **Don't blow it!** Now that you have their attention, they may invite you to their table to introduce them to their guests. Now don't blow it! Sure, you're in but don't get overconfident. Keep an eye on the clock and on your drink. Try to keep it to a drink and hour. As the night gets later, you will see the very successful always keep their wits about them.

- **ALWAYS have a business card on you.** It should either be a personal card that has nothing but your name and contact information or one from you work. I personally carry two types of cards. One card for my adventures, book, world travel, etc. And the second card would be for whatever my "real" job is. Depending on how I might want to stand apart or possibly try to fit in depends on what card I give them.

You Never Know Who You Will Meet at a VIP Party

Who will you meet at a VIP party or on a super yacht? You never know who might show up, but this I *can* promise you for sure: you will meet amazing people with amazing stories. Everything from running from lions in Africa to super stars coming to dinner to meet their grandma. No matter who you are with, if they are at a VIP party I am sure they have a good story to tell.

If they do not have something interesting it's not that they do not know of anything fun or fanciful to say, it's just that they do not trust you yet. So get their attention, make them think or ask them a question. In no time they'll be opening up to you for sure.

One question I ask every successful person I meet, "If you could give advice to yourself at age (insert your age) what would it be?" Half of the time they kinda laugh and say something like, "You're a smart kid," the other half start to think hard. You can see it draws emotions they have not felt in years. This helps portray a companionship where they will lower their guard and you will stand out from the rest of the party goers.

Specifically, here are the various types of VIP folks you meet at these exclusive-parties in mega-yachts:

- **Pro Athletes** – you will meet a number of pro athletes. Now, they may not have money but their sponsors do and are making sure to show it off at this event.

- **Super Models** – super models are a great bragging point for anyone at a party. They sometimes can be very um boring but they look very good and command attention. Remember, the owner is spending all this money for attention, so give it to them.

- **CEOs** – Big money brings in big money. If you have a nice VIP party during something like a film festival, you will have the investors for these big films come to the same party. There are there to see how their money is being spent and who they can meet or make a deal with.

- **Celebrities** – What would be better than a supermodel at your party than someone like George Clooney or Angelina Jolie? The celebrities are friends with the high rollers because each can benefit the other in one way or another. Attention is the key in this game, always trying to promote or meet the next big deal.

- **Royalty** – Yes, I have meet Princes and Princesses in a number of parties. Whatever you do, don't laugh when introduced as his holiness Prince Fazza (crowned prince of Dubai.)At these parties you will never know who you are meeting. They might be in jeans and a T-shirt and have not shaved. Just keep any eye out and never be afraid to ask questions.

Where to Start Your VIP Adventure

I've had the best luck at sponsored events, yacht parties, races, dances, and fundraisers, but really anyplace the rich and powerful gather, you can find some kind of event going on. Whether you are at the Kentucky Derby or the Cannes film festival, there will always be a party. If you truly wish to meet a celebrity or maybe a pro athlete, plan your mission around the events they attend. Here's how:

- **Find the date and time of the event.** It could be the Pro Bowl, or a movie festival in Cannes, France, or a premier in Barcelona, Spain. You can Google the information you need and then act accordingly.

- **Zero in.** Try to stay in the same town as the event and get a hotel that is as close to the event as possible.

- **Ask around.** Once you get checked in, circulate, mingle, and talk to people. Sure enough, someone will all know where the biggest party of the night is. So then just walk past that event, or act like you belong and just walk right in. When it comes to crashing a party, remember that the worst thing they can say is "no."

- **Always keep a good attitude.** Word to the wise: no matter how good your VIP game is, you will not always get in to the best party of the night. Be prepared to get all dressed up walk around for an hour and not get into any party. It happens, but try to make the best of it. Case in point:

I was once invited to a party on Paul Allen's yacht in Cannes, France. But the boat that picks you up to bring you to the party had to move due to the French police claiming they were too noisy. I was devastated because I really wanted to attend this party.

But I kept a positive attitude and on my walk home I met another guy was there waiting for the

same boat. We went out for dinner and ran into
someone who invited us into his little party instead.

At that same table where two very big name TV
personalities. It was an amazing night. Even though
we didn't get on the yacht, staying positive allowed
me to find another party and still network that night.
And to this day I am still friends with those people.

Parting Words:
Making the Most of Your (Temporary) VIP Status

As you can see, it takes a little work to get
into these VIP parties. But take it from me, it's totally
worth it. If you make just one connection at each
party, think of the opportunities that lie in your path.

And even if you only make one connection
every few parties, you're still better off than hanging
out with the same folks in the same bar every night.
Sure, it takes a little more work to get spruced up,
play the game and crash the party, but the payoff is
well worth it.

Whatever you do, or wherever you do it, make
sure to make the most out of your temporary VIP
status. Remember that you are in a position lots of
your friends back home would kill for, and never
forget where you are.

Chapter 8:
Get Ready For Your Own Epic Adventure

There you have it, a host of great ideas, tips, strategies, and tactics for not only getting around the world, free or paid, but meeting folks who might help you once you get back home.

You have heard my stories and adventures, all of which are true. I have had to rely on God for his mercy and grace over and over again for protection. After traveling for ten months, being almost broke with nowhere to stay, I received a call not even twenty minutes after being robbed; it was a writer, who offered me a place to stay. She was leaving for Iceland for the next three weeks and as long as I would walk her dog, I could stay as long as I wished.

Living large takes a different kind of person. I would go from a super yacht in Monaco then walk back to my tent for the night. But I promise if you choose this adventure, you will have amazing epic highs but, remember, they come with lows just as large. You will have a dinner for three thousand dollars, and then wake up in the morning and not have enough money for a sandwich, so you only buy the bread. This is how my life was and I would not change it for a second.

I can't tell you how much fun I've had on my own epic adventures, and how eager I am to get back out there and explore the world one more time – or one hundred and one more times!

These are adventures people would never ever imagine they could go on. But you will never know what might happen that night unless you get out and try, TRY to sneak into that party, TRY to meet new people. Just get out there because, remember, your chance of success is a guaranteed zero percent if you do not even try. And never be afraid to fail. Instead, keep a smile on your face and good attitude because sometimes your failure is better than if you were to succeed in the first place.

But now it's time for us to part ways so that you can get busy getting ready for your own epic adventure. Whether it's crewing a mega yacht across the Atlantic Ocean or simply hopping a flight to some exotic destination and working your way back home – no matter how long that might take – there is a big, wide world out there to explore and I wish you the best of luck doing so.

Before I leave you, here are some simple, quick tips to live by on your own epic adventure across the world, or simply across town:

- **Keep an open mind.** Obviously, if you're open to traveling the world this first one may not be the biggest problem for you. But, I've seen lots of Americans who say they want to "travel the world and try new things," and the minute they land in port they're upset because they can't find a good cheeseburger or TV station. Creature comforts are great, but all that stuff will still be waiting for you when you get back home. Instead, keep an open mind on your travels so you'll be open to trying new things, meeting new people and going new places, even if they're slightly out of your usual comfort zone.

- **Keep a journal.** This book started from the blog I kept at www.trekkingwithtrav.com. Every day or so I would chronicle my journeys, upload the posts to my blog and carry on with my day. A few people saw it, got interested and reached out to me to ask, "Hey, have you ever thought about writing a book?" Heck no I hadn't, but now I have and the same can happen for you. Having a blog, website, Facebook page or Instagram account where you upload words or pictures from your daily travels can help you secure.

- **Keep your wits about you.** Whatever you do, wherever you go, stay safe. Think sharp, look lively and remember that it's always good to have a buddy system when going out to new places in a new town.

- **Keep your eyes open.** Finally, enjoy yourself. Souvenirs are great and blogs are grand but the best experiences are those we see with our eyes and feel with our hearts. Watch, listen and learn as you travel the world, because souvenirs can get lost or broken in transit, but memories last a lifetime.

- **Be spontaneous** – If you have never traveled and have little funds look into the last minute deals on any travel web site. I caught a flight to Costa Rica from Michigan USA for $160.Once I landed, I asked the cab driver what was going on in the town. He said a massive ISDE surf tournament was two hours outside the city. I went there and rented a hammock (for $4 a night) behind a burger shop since all the rooms where full. I ate cheap (PB&J, or rice and beans), went surfing, snorkeling, and walked around the city. The entire trip cost me a TOTAL of four hundred dollars. This is a budget that anyone can afford. So get start go travel.

- **Look into the feature.** Even though you are on this party/adventure just keep an open mind to what you will be doing when you get home. During this adventure I meet some amazing people and even had a job offer with close to seven-figure income. This job would be in a hostel incitement in a mine in a remote area of china half the year and a remote mine in Africa the second part of the year. I passed on this, but also was offered a six-figure income in Dubai for a web page as there sales manager. These are both positions you don't get offered when you graduate college. There are only things you will hear about once you meet the owner and when he likes you. Keep that in mind you never know who you will meet or what will happen once you get home. You might wake up one morning with a job offer in your Facebook message box.

Thanks again for following along on my adventures, and have fun on your own. While I'm thinking about it, I sure would love to hear how you're making out. Be sure to drop by my web page and send an email maybe someday we can meet up on an adventure.

Feel free to visit trekkingwithtrav.com and drop me a line so I can see where you are, and you can see where I am. Speaking of, my next adventures include a ride through romaine ending in Transylvania. I will also be going on some mini adventures in South America and am looking forward to traveling to Antarctica before I am thirty to complete all seven continents. I will also be on tour traveling the United States speaking with universities as well as select high schools, so if your university would like me to speak with them, please feel free to contact my people at PartyLikeaBillionaire.com.

No matter how many people say that your dream is impossible, no matter how many travel agents start laughing at you on the phone because of your budget, ignore them, dig deep, and push through. Some of the most amazing people and experiences you will ever find are just around the corner. Remember, your chances for success and adventure drastically increase once you try.